PENNY STOCKS:

Exactly How to Find Penny Stocks That Can Make You MILLIONS in The Stock Market...

Sofia Martinez

Wait! Before You Proceed… Have You Ever Invested in Penny Stocks?

If you want to learn Penny Stock investing, you need to start at the top. Now, these aren't for everyone, but is you want access to the FREE report highlighting the EXACT resources we've used to build our portfolios visit:

PennyStockResource.org

TABLE OF CONTENTS

Introduction

I want to sincerely thank you and congratulate you for downloading this book.

It contains proven steps and strategies on how you can make money in penny stocks.

Everyone wants to achieve financial freedom. People want a life well-lived without having to worry about money. This can actually be achieved but it takes a lot of discipline and focus. A lot of books and articles have been written about different methods to earn money. This book is one of them.

You'll learn a lot of concepts about penny stocks through this book. Although there are some critics to this type of investment, it isn't necessarily bad if you try to learn about it and decide later if you want to dabble in it. What's important is that you have the willingness to learn about penny stocks.

Thanks again for downloading this book, I hope you enjoy it!

Sofia

Chapter 1: What Is A Penny Stock?

Previously, a penny stock is a stock which is traded for at most $1 per share. However, the Securities and Exchange Commission in the United States of America has changed the definition to include every stock which trades below $5 per share. Even if a penny stock is currently traded for more than its original price, it's still considered a penny stock because it is still a very risky investment.

In general, a growing company, with limited resources and cash, offers a penny stock to investors. The stock generates low trading volumes because investors don't give it much attention. It is often traded on Pink Sheets and Over-the-counter Bulletin Board. A penny stock is a primary target of market manipulations, which can't be used in stocks traded on the stock market. Therefore, investors must exercise caution when trading penny stocks. It is true that these stocks can generate huge returns but it can also bring about huge losses.

In some countries, a penny stock is referred to as a cent stock. A small public company can offer a cent stock as its common shares. However, the US Securities & Exchange Commission defines this type of stock as a security which is traded less than $5 per share, doesn't meet other criteria set by SEC, and isn't publicly traded on a stock exchange. In the UK, a penny share is a stock which is priced below £1.

A penny stock has low market capitalization. It can be subject to manipulation and pump and dump scams. It is also highly volatile and presents a huge amount of risk to investors. In the US, the Financial Industry Regulatory Authority and the SEC have guidelines and rules to define and regulate its sale.

Why Investors Need To Be Worried

A penny stock, especially the one which trades below $0.01, is often thinly traded. Manipulators and stock promoters often use it for its pump and dump scheme. They initially buy the bulk of this stock then inflate its share price through misleading and false statements.

A pump and dump scheme is fraudulent. Some organizations or individuals buy penny stock shares and use email blasts, fake press releases, stock message boards, chat rooms, and websites to generate interest to the stock. In most cases, a person will claim to have a hot tip about a particular penny stock in order to persuade naïve investors to buy the shares quickly. When more investors buy the shares, the price will shoot up to entice more investors to purchase the shares. In the end, the manipulators will sell all their shares and earn huge profits from them.

For example, rapper 50 Cent used Twitter to dramatically increase the price of HNHI, a penny stock. He owned 30 million shares and was able to earn $8.7 million from the sale. Another example is the case of Lithium Exploration Group whose market capitalization went up to at least $350 million after the company executed an extensive mail campaign. In a 10-Q form the company filed on December 31, 2010, it listed the firm with no assets and zero revenues. After the promotion, it bought lithium exploration properties to address the concerns of the press.

In some cases, a company can do a pump and dump when it wants to promote its stock. In general, the price of the penny stock moves due to momentum. It is volatile because of the spread and the way the Securities and Exchange Commission regulates it. The SEC can halt the trading when it notices that its price has gone up very fast. Until such time that it is released by SEC again, the price of the penny can move either way and investors don't have control over their shares.

Regulating the Trade of Penny Stocks

In the United States of America, a penny stock must meet various standards like minimum shareholder equity, market capitalization, and price. A publicly-listed stock, which is traded on the stock exchange, isn't regulated like a penny stock even though its price is below $5. It is classified as a low-priced stock and not as a penny stock.

The Financial Industry Regulatory Authority and the Securities and Exchange Commission control penny stock trading through their rules and regulations. The State of Georgia was the first to enact a comprehensive penny stock law. After the law was upheld by the US District Court, the SEC and the FINRA made comprehensive revisions on their regulations, which were effective in restricting or closing dealers and brokers. However, pump and dump schemes by unregistered individuals and groups have not been addressed by these regulations.

Chapter 2: The Bright Side and the Scary Side of Penny Stocks

Can you really turn 'pennies' into fortunes? You bet! The internet is teeming with these rags to riches stories. These *'pennies to fortune'* stories reveal the exploits of penny stock traders who built their fortune trading penny stocks. Even the mainstream media has been adding up to the hype created by these stories by featuring choice penny stocks regularly on their financial news sections. They have in fact reserved special sections exclusively for featured penny stocks.

However, not all of these stories are hype. Quite a number of these *'pennies to fortune'* stories have been confirmed to be true. Others could be doubtful though especially those bandied around by brokers who have vested interests in drumming up interest for the services they offer. Never the less, the few confirmed success stories point to an undeniable fact – people can make a fortune by trading penny stocks.

There could even be more of these successful penny stock stories that never saw print or reached broadcast media. And, there is little chance we will ever get to hear them at all. You see, the bulk of investors particularly the successful ones belong to a secretive lot. They regard their successful trading sorties with utmost confidentiality. They would rather keep their trading secrets closed to their chests and their earnings stashed away in some secret bank accounts. You won't read or hear about their profitable exploits much less discover the details of how they built their fortunes with mere pennies. They regard their exploits as well-guarded secrets that naturally they won't easily share with the universe.

But hey, if you come to think of it, there are really no secrets to penny stock trading success. Success comes from pure hard work and from having a logical and keenly analytical mind with a head full of common sense, and a crystal clear knowledge of every penny stock being offered for trade. Success in trading penny stocks involves developing a deep appreciation and understanding of the underlying risks involved with trading undervalued penny stocks. All these are what draw the line between penny stock millionaires who were able to build their fortunes and those who lost theirs.

If you wish to tread the same silvery path taken by these self-made penny stock millionaires, you need to have a deep understanding of what penny stocks are. You need to be able to dig up, identify, analyze, and project the potential of all the underlying fundamentals that may potentially cause their prices to rise or fall.

To begin with, let us review once more w*hat Penny Stocks are?*

As mentioned earlier in this book, you won't really find stocks that are worth pennies nowadays. What penny stocks refer to today are the shares of companies offered for sale at $5 per or less each.

The Securities and Exchange Commission has a more definitive explanation of what a penny stock is. They describe penny stocks as company shares that have share values of $5 or less each and are not listed in any of the major stock exchanges.

You may want to ask - 'if they are not listed in any of the major stock exchanges, where and how are they traded then?'

Penny stocks are shares of minimally capitalized companies. They are low priced stocks which do not meet federal regulatory and financial reporting requirements and therefore do not qualify to be listed for trading in any of the stock exchanges. Instead, they are traded via over-the-counter bulletin boards (OTCBB) or through what they call as 'pink sheets'. Trading is decentralized and done through a broker or a middleman who consummates the deals equipped only with a table and a telephone much like during the early days of stock trading. The way penny stock transactions are conducted have not really changed much since those days.

The only thing that changed is the fact the term 'penny stock' has become a misnomer. The reference to the *penny* is actually misleading since there are no more stocks today with a penny per share value. Although occasionally, you may find some stocks trading well below $1 per share, still you won't find one that costs a penny.

Please note too that the current definition of penny stocks does excludes stocks that are listed in the major exchanges like NASDAQ and NYSE whose values may have fallen below $5 per share (even if many investors prefer to refer to any and all $5 shares as penny stocks).

The 'Wild West of Wall Street' is how some pundits describe penny stock trading because it represents the untamed world of investing – decentralized and hardly regulated. Here, the volume of trade is so low that some moneyed investors can easily manipulate prices. Try to watch the movie 'Wolf of Wall Street' and you will understand exactly what I mean. The movie reveals the ugly side of penny stock trading. It is so decentralized that scammers and corrupt brokers out to make their fast buck at the expense of unsuspecting investors has made it their home.

You will find shares of companies who don't meet the strict listing requirements of the SEC and the major exchanges posted instead at the OTCBB or on pink sheets. These two are the only options the said companies have to get their stocks offered for sale to the investing public. (OTCBB has less stringent requirements than the major exchanges while pink sheets don't have any such requirements and shares don't even have to be registered with the SEC).

It goes without saying therefore that OTCBB stocks and pink sheet stocks are high-risk investments. Value investors avoid them mainly because of their low liquidity that often results in extreme price volatility. More often than not, prices are manipulated. Because of the low liquidity, you may find it difficult to buy a stock at your desired price just as it will be difficult to liquidate your position if and when you want to get out. It is a sellers' market where the one offering the stocks dictates the price. Sadly, this is the scary side of penny stocks.

On the bright side, it is only in the OTCBB and pink sheets where you can stumble upon promising startups with small caps many of them are just waiting for their big breaks before their stocks start to soar. Here, you will discover startup companies with unique and innovative products whose patents are pending approval. Here, you will also find small cap companies that are still in the process of merging or being acquired by much larger companies, which can boost their market value after the merger or acquisition pushes through. Then there are companies whose potential values can suddenly soar because of some recent dramatic developments in the industry to which they belong.

Never forget that any positive news that directly impacts the potential growth of small cap companies can easily propel the stocks of the said companies to rise to unprecedented heights, and can even cause their stocks to graduate into the major leagues of stock trading. This is where penny stock traders make their fortunes. This is the bright side of penny stock trading.

The challenge to penny stock traders lie in how successful they can filter out the crappy stocks from those whose values are about to soar while remaining unintimidated by the din and the confusion that surrounds a decentralized, highly volatile, and extremely risky market.

Chapter 3: Risks and Potential of Penny Stocks Investing

Investing in penny stocks can be very risky but it also has a great potential to generate significant returns. However, it must be noted that a lot of people gamble on penny stocks and significant returns can be generated over the short term. A lot of companies offering penny stocks are usually overleveraged or headed towards bankruptcy. Some of these corporations are also shell companies which scammers use to dupe other people.

The Risks of Penny Stocks Trading

In most cases, penny stocks are traded on Over-the-counter Bulletin Board or Pink Sheets. An investor will find challenging to search for information about the companies offering their stocks on the OTCBB so he will find it difficult to make a logical conclusion about a particular company. In addition, for both Pink Sheets and OTCBB, there is a lack of credible sources about these stocks. In fact, listing on either exchange doesn't even require a company to meet some minimum standards.

Furthermore, there is a lot of liquidity in trading penny stocks. It may be possible to buy a penny stock but disposing the shares will pose a problem because the trading volume is very low. This means that the investor will find it difficult to sell his penny stock even if he wants to lock in his profits because there are fewer interested buyers at the target price. The investor will then have to wait for a willing buyer or sell the stock at a lower price. If the person decides to wait, he may find himself trapped in a pump-and-dump scheme and sees even his capital being wiped out. If he decides to lower the price, he will see a reduction in his profits.

Lastly, there are so many scammers offering biased tips about a particular penny stock. A potential investor may receive brochures through email or snail mail. The material usually contains some hyped-up claims that the specific penny stock will experience significant gains because of a revolutionary technology. The unsuspecting individual doesn't know that the person or company sending the brochures is just selling his own shares at discounted prices.

The Potential of Penny Stock

To make money with penny stocks, an individual must go along with the pump-and-dump scheme. This means that he buys the stock when he receives the spam email or junk mail then wait for the other people to buy it also so that the trading volume will be increased. However, the investor must sell his shares quickly to lock in his small profits. Timing is crucial with this kind of strategy. If he misses the initial surge in trading volume, he may eventually lose all his capital.

Another strategy is to list all penny stocks and perform due diligence on companies which have generated revenues, offered liquid stocks, and operated a legitimate website with company images and contact information. In addition, these companies must have a strong balance sheet or is debt-free, and have reduced losses or remained profitable.

Why Is A Penny Stock A Risky Investment?

First, the public has no access to all information. To be successful in investing, an investor must have enough tangible information to help him make a good decision. Those companies listed on Pink Sheets don't file with SEC so they aren't regulated or scrutinized publicly. In addition, most information about these companies isn't credible.

Second, Pink Sheets and Over-the-counter Bulletin Board don't require companies to meet some minimum standard requirements. It is possible for a company to be listed on these exchanges because it failed to maintain its position on the major exchange. The OTCBB requires listed companies to at least file SEC documents on a timely manner. However, Pink Sheets doesn't have any requirement.

Third, most listed companies in OTCBB and Pink Sheets are either nearing bankruptcy or newly created. Thus, these companies may have no track record at all. It is very difficult to determine the potential of a penny stock if the company doesn't have historical information.

Fourth, penny stocks have liquidity problems. It is possible that an investor won't be able to dispose his stock because he can't find a willing buyer for it. He may even be forced to lower his price if he wants to sell it immediately. Furthermore, some unscrupulous individuals and companies may manipulate the price of a penny stock through pump and dump scheme.

Penny Stock Scams

A penny stock can pose problems not only to the investor but to the Securities and Exchange Commission as well. Its poor liquidity and lack of information make it an easy target for scammers.

Some penny stock companies pay persons to recommend the stock using various media like radio shows, newsletters, and financial television. An investor may receive a spam email informing him of a great earning opportunity. It is best for the person to check if the people recommending the stock are being paid for their services.

It is also possible for an investor to be scammed by offshore brokers. The SEC allows companies to sell stocks to foreign investors offshore without the need to register the stocks. What these companies do is that they sell their shares of stock at a discount to foreign buyers, who then sell them back to investors in the United States of America at a higher price. These offshore brokers often make cold calls to potential investors and offer hot tips to entice them to buy the stock.

The Fallacy of the Penny Stock

Unsuspecting investors are made to believe that a lot of currently popular stocks started out as penny stocks. They believed that today's large companies only appreciated in values. By performing due diligence, an investor will realize that companies like Wal-Mart and Microsoft had been reduced to pennies because of stock splits. These companies didn't start their businesses at a low market price.

Lastly, a lot of investors become attracted to penny stocks because they believe that these stocks will appreciate and offer more opportunities. For example, a $0.10 share price, which appreciates to $0.15, has made a 50% profit. Therefore, a $1,000 investment is able to buy 10,000 shares and earns $500 after the increase in value. Investors fail to realize that if it's possible to earn $500 from the transaction, it is also possible to lose $500 or all of the capital.

Chapter 4: How to Invest In Penny Stocks

Open a Trading Account

When an investor opens a trading account, he must consider customer service, fees, and how quickly funds can be transferred. There are brokers with various specializations so it is best for him to shop around for an account which matches his requirements.

A penny stock investor must be very concerned about the broker's fee structure. There are brokers who charge commissions per share, which is a scheme with a fixed rate for a minimum number of shares. They also charge another rate for succeeding shares. This fee structure is for an investor who has low capital. For penny stock traders, it is more cost-effective to search for a broker who offers a low flat rate per transaction. With a low fee, the trader can generate more money because of less commissions and fees.

Where to Find Penny Stocks

Penny stocks are traded at the Over-the-counter Bulletin Board and Pink Sheets because listing in major exchanges require special requirements.

Choosing Penny Stocks from the List

There are different ways to pick a penny stock. Some brokers and websites offer stock screening tools which help an investor narrow down the list based on his risk tolerance and strategy.

Don't Indulge into a Mindless Buying Spree

Never get into a mindless buying binge simply because penny stocks are so cheap as compared to regular stocks. You may end up tying your capital to a portfolio of worthless, non-performing assets. Penny stock trading is truly attractive to investors you can build a diverse investment portfolio using very little capital. The temptation to go on a buying binge can be overwhelming. However, you have to exercise some restraint and incorporate some discipline into your trading to make good money. The success of your penny stock trading journey hinges on picking the right stock as it is about to take off. It means you have to do exhaustive research otherwise you may end up losing a fortune if you just pick them up at random.

How to do it? Always study the underlying fundamentals.

You have to know the stock well enough before you buy them. This is basic to stock trading, in case you have forgotten. There is no way you envision the future prospects of a company and the industry it belongs to if you have not scrutinized diligently every single fundamental factor underlying the company. You will also not be able to forecast the full potential for growth of the company if you are not aware of the state of the industry it belongs to. If your aim is to build a robust retirement kitty from the small money you are ready to invest then you have to pour a great deal of your time and effort doing due diligence before pouring money on penny stocks. It doesn't make sense to gamble away your money by investing it as if you are placing a bet on a roulette or black jack table – even if you can afford it. In the first place, the main reason you are investing your money on stocks is to make some profit and build a treasure trove you can bank on for the rainy days. Keep in mind that you are not here to lose money.

There is no cutting corners here. You have to dig out information and try to know enough about the penny stock you are planning to buy and its potential value in the future before you let those pennies fly out of your pocket. Don't buy them simply because they are cheap. That's the most obvious thing about penny stocks. You have to take it a step farther analyze why they are cheap as well as determine the current status of the company and the industry it belongs to. It is not going to be easy but it's the only way to avoid buying lemons for the stocks.

No matter how small the money you are putting on the line is, you still have to do exhaustive studies and know enough about the company and its industry before you zip open your pockets. If you want to be another penny stock millionaire, you need to do what others did to make those millions.

Can you imagine buying into a biotech company when you don't have any idea about the industry or about what is currently the state of the biotech industry – just because it is cheap? The best-case scenario is you get your money tied up to it for a long while. The worst-case scenario – you lose everything you have invested in it.

On the other hand, if you've done your due diligence and saw bright prospects in the future for the company whose stocks you are thinking of buying, then you are in the right track. Remember that the more successful penny traders picked their stock choices based on careful analysis and not from random choices.

Understanding the Risk

A penny stock is very volatile. Putting money in it may result to substantial gains but there is a greater probability of suffering from losses. As such, it is important for any investor to be cautious about trading penny stocks. Money managers, mutual funds, and index funds have set rules to follow so they can't trade penny stocks. Therefore, only a few investors place their money in penny stocks. It is important to note that the issue of liquidity can't be ignored. A retail investor may get stuck with a penny stock for a long time if there is not enough supply and demand for him to trade his stock.

Chapter 5: Avoiding Penny Stock Scams

We have said it before and we are saying it again here as a warning to all penny stock millionaire *want-to-be* not to fall for any penny stock scams perpetrated by scrupulous brokers. There are a lot of these scams happening right now.

Penny stock trading as we said before is decentralized and transactions are hardly regulated so much so that it has become the haven and the favorite hunting ground of scam artists out to rob unsuspecting investors of their hard earned money.

One of the more common scams which scrupulous brokers still play on unsuspecting investors is called *'pump and dump'*. It involves the use of high pressure tactics to convince people to buy chunks of useless stocks which these brokers have earlier put their stake on - buying these worthless stocks at pennies to a share early on. They would then come up with hyped up stories to tell unsuspecting victims about some stocks whose value is about to soar. The idea is to generate enough interest for their worthless stocks to induce a buying frenzy. Naturally, the ensuing buying interest for the stocks pushes the prices high enough for the brokers to start unloading their stake with a nifty profit. As the brokers start to sell their stake, the price of the stock then take a dramatic plunge leaving the poor investors in the cold nursing huge losses and with no recourse but walk away with their pockets empty.

Such a scenario was depicted in a recent movie entitled The Wolf of Wall Street which is actually based on the true to life story of a broker named Mr. Belfort (portrayed by Leonardo Di Carpio in the movie). *If you haven't seen the movie yet, I suggest you buy a DVD and watch it at home. It is a real eye-opener for people who are thinking of investing on penny stocks.* It reveals how scam artists operate and watching the movie will teach you enough to avoid them.

Anyway, the scam perpetrated by Mr. Belfort in that movie continues to be played on unsuspecting investors by scrupulous brokers over and over again. Worst, whose lot continue to increase through time. The 'pump and dump' scam is not just movie stuff. Every day, there is such a scam happening in the universe. Take for example one of the more recent scams perpetrated by some brokers to promote the stocks of the unheard of microcap H&H Imports. These brokers paid the popular rapper 50 cents to entice his over

3.8 million Twitter followers to buy the stocks of H&H Imports. Because of his tweets, the price of the stock rose dramatically by 208% giving the brokers who owned the stocks prior to 50 cents' tweets - a hefty profit.

There are other microcap scams that are continually being perpetrated on penny stock investors. You should be familiar with them so you can avoid risking your money by putting it in such dubious schemes.

There are other penny stock scams you need to be aware of, Here are some of them:

- Bait and Switch – this dubious scheme uses fancy advertising heralding promising returns on stocks in a highly active and fast developing industry which is presently in the limelight to lure unsuspecting investors. But after the client makes contact, he is promptly informed that the stocks are all gone. He is instead offered some other worthless stocks which these brokers have previously purchased at pennies per share.

- Chop Stocks – These are stocks that were previously bought cheap which were given to brokers to be sold scandalously high prices. Because of the huge commissions they will get, these brokers dump these stocks in the laps of unsuspecting investors using high handed tactics once again.

- Dump and dilute – This is a scam perpetrated by the small cap company itself. This dubious scheme involves continuously issuing of shares by the company to raise more money from new investors. As more and more shares are issued, the value of the stocks of the previous investors gets diluted. Not only that because you can expect that this company will next do a reverse stock split which will ultimately leave investors with a net loss.

- Not net sales policy – This is a scheme where investors are prevented from or discouraged from selling their stocks.

We won't be surprised if there are more penny stock scams out there other than those we have mentioned. There is really there is no way you can put a plug to these scams as penny stock trading remains decentralized and slightly regulated. Besides, scam artists and professional swindlers will always try to look for weaknesses in the system they can exploit to defraud investors of their money.

The is no better way to minimize your risks and avoid these scams than to equip yourself with enough knowledge about how these scams are perpetrated so you can avoid falling prey to them once they start knocking on your door. To make the story short, the best way penny stock would-be millionaires can avoid being scammed by these scam artists to totally shut the door on them. It means you should shun away from unsolicited investment advice. Furthermore, you should rely more on your own abilities to conduct your own due diligence prior to your stock picking activities. Discard those stocks being hyped by various media outlets this means they do not rely on media hype and avoid relying on the published and broadcasted financial news in making your penny stock picks.

Chapter 6: How to Spot Winning Penny Stocks

Not all stocks listed on the OTCBB will get listed to a major stock exchange. Most companies will be bankrupt or vanish into oblivion even before they profit from their products and services. However, the trading volume of OTCBB still continues its phenomenal growth. About 650 billion shares have been traded in 2006. Majority of penny stock companies have no revenues or profits. However, it is possible for traders to learn how to choose a company which is likely to succeed.

Making Probability Work

A penny stock investor must know what type of company he's looking for. In addition, he must also possess the appropriate tools to help him look for the best stock. Since the average price of a penny stock is $0.10, it will be best to search for stocks priced between $0.05 and $2. If the investor wants to search for a higher-priced penny stock, he may find fewer stocks.

He must search for penny stocks with at least 100,000 shares of average daily volume. The focus must be on those stocks which are on an uptrend. Therefore, the trader can use the positive 3-week and 10-week price data, and with the 9-day simple moving average greater than its 18-day counterpart. The trader can exclude companies with negative earnings growth rates or negative earnings per share. He must focus on stocks on an uptrend for at least a 5-day period. He must be interested in stocks which are frequently on an uptrend.

Each penny stock must pass the news, short interest, and visual tests. A healthy chart pattern is required. It must show that the price is on an uptrend and moving above the support levels. To pass the news test, the penny stock company must generate positive news in order to attract more investors. A short interest is a percentage of the total shares which had been sold short but hadn't been closed yet. If this percentage is higher than 5%, it can mean trouble. However, if this percentage continues to increase, it will push the price even higher.

Choosing the Winners

A retail investor may commit one of his biggest trading mistakes if he sees a penny stock as something which is affordable. He believes that he will earn more money if he buys more shares of one penny stock instead of buying shares of a higher-priced stock listed on a major exchange. Although it may seem rational, it is important that he doesn't overlook the number of shares outstanding.

For example, companies A and B have $100,000,000 market capitalization each. If the share price of company A is $0.10, it means that its number of shares outstanding is equal to 1,000,000,000. On the other hand, if company B's share price is $100, its number of shares outstanding is 1,000,000. Therefore, before company A gets fully capitalized, it needs investors to buy the 1,000,000,000 shares. It is easier to sell 1,000,000 shares at $100 than 1,000,000,000 shares at $0.10.

An investor must also be aware of dilution of penny stocks. This means that a stock's number of shares outstanding may grow out of control by using employee stock options, stock splits, and share issuance to increase capitalization. If the company issues more shares, ownership percentage of investors will be diluted. Therefore, if an investor wants to be successful in penny stocks, he must be able to search for a company which has very strong share structure so that existing owners won't see the value of their investment eroded by continuous dilution.

Spotting the Best Penny Stock

Penny stock companies have low market capitalizations. Anyone, who wants to invest in them, must consider the fundamentals of these companies. He must know about their share structure, competition, and underlying fundamentals so that he'll be able to determine the best possible stock to invest in.

The investor must also know the sectors where these penny stocks belong. Most penny stocks are in the mining and metals sector. Aggressive incentive plans, increased competition, and fund operations must be considered if he wants to earn more profits from these penny stocks.

Using Financial Ratios to Determine the Winning Stock

If a penny stock company is able to provide adequate financial disclosure, the investor can perform analysis to determine if it is worth investing in it. If there's a positive trend and strong numbers on the financial statements, he will be able to foretell the future expectations of performance of the penny stock company.

The Liquidity Ratios

These ratios are used to compute for penny stocks since most of them are unable to pay for their short-term debts. If the liquidity ratio is low, it means that the penny stock company is advancing its operations or struggling to remain in business.

The Leverage Ratios

Leverage ratios are similar to liquidity ratios. Both of them focus on the ability of the penny stock company to pay off its debts. However, with leverage ratios, the concern is on long-term debt.

$$Debt\ Ratio = \frac{Total\ Liabilities}{Total\ Assets}$$

If the debt load is expanding, the company is supporting its business development and future growth opportunities.

$$Interest\ Coverage\ Ratio = \frac{Earnings\ Before\ Interest\ and\ Taxes}{Interest\ Expense}$$

The interest coverage ratio is used to know if the debts are still manageable and if the company can pay off its outstanding debts from its earnings level. If this ratio results to a number less than 2, it means the company is will experience problems with its long-term debts.

The Performance Ratio

The performance ratio quantifies the revenues generated by the company through its income statement. It is important for a penny stock company to show consistent earnings growth.

The Valuation Ratios

Valuation ratios measure the penny stock's attractiveness at its present price. In general, it is possible for a penny stock to be significantly overvalued. An investor can use these ratios as tools to find out if a particular stock is overvalued or undervalued.

$$Price\text{-}to\text{-}Earnings\ Ratio = \frac{Current\ Share\ Price}{Earnings\ Per\ Share}$$

This ratio doesn't mean anything if there is zero or negative company earnings. If it results to a low ratio, it means that the company is able to provide better value per its dollar of earnings.

$$Price\text{-}to\text{-}Sales\ Ratio = \frac{Current\ Share\ Price}{Sales\ Per\ Share}$$

A Price-to-Sales Ratio result of 2 or less means that the share value is good.

$$Price\text{-}to\text{-}Cash\ Flow\ Ratio = \frac{Current\ Share\ Price}{Total\ Cash\ Flow\ Per\ Share}$$

As a variation of Price-to-Sales Ratio, this ratio is used to determine if the earnings are of good quality or not.

Chapter 7: How to Find Companies with Future Value

Penny stock trading can be described simply as targeted stock picking. It involves a continuous process of looking for companies whose stocks have the potential to soar in the near term. In effect what you will be looking for are companies with the following attributes:

- Have an efficient management staff,

- With promising product innovation,

- Have a progressively decreasing debt load,

- Consistently increasing revenue,

- Plus other positive factors that reflects the company has a dynamic management staff.

In penny stock trading, it is the quality and the timing of your stock picks which will determine whether you make money or lose money with each pick. Basically, you will be looking for companies whose future value appears to be headed nowhere else but north.

The idea is to filter out the pink elephants and limit your choices to a few promising penny stocks which have the highest percentage of making a turnaround based on the current status and the most recent developments in the respective industries. Off hand, let me tell you that it is not going to be an easy task. It may even take you quite a bit of time list down at least ten promising penny stocks. It will be next to impossible to come with such a list in just a short time since you have to sift through thousands of available penny stocks not to mention the fact that you also have to scrutinize the financial records of each and every one of them.

Don't lose heart though because there are simple ways to come up with a list of preferred penny stock picks. For starters, here are some helpful hints on what and where to look for penny stocks with great potential for growth:

- Look for bankrupt companies which are in the process of undergoing restructuring or being bought by another company. Having gone through bankruptcy their stocks must be dirt cheap. Now scrutinize the restructuring plans and look for any indications or sign that the company may be able to settle their debt soon. Look at their list of valuable assets. There may be something there that is attractive enough to lure other companies to purchase this company thereby increasing its chances of making a recovery in the near term. Or, you can look at the financial history of the company - for all you know, the company just needs extra attention in some aspects of their operation to get back in contention.

- You can try taking a long shot by sifting through the mesh of available penny stock companies every now and then. You may be able to find some really undervalued penny stocks ready to graduate into the majors. It is a fact that the market can get weird at times and undervalues some stocks. Just keep searching and your effort may just pay off.

- Give special attention to IPOs or Initial Public Offerings of small companies particularly those that have unique products and those that employ cutting edge technology. For all you know these companies may just not have the resources to make a huge initial public offering and are thus forced to make their initial offerings much like penny stocks. Never the less, they are not only good bargains but they will also help you establish your investment portfolio using very minimal capital.

Chapter 8: Effective Strategies for Day-Trading Penny Stocks

For the past decade, penny stock has continuously gained popularity. A lot of traders, who made significant profits from trading penny stocks, use day-trading strategies. With day-trading, an investor doubles his capital within a short period of time. Furthermore, he can trade volumes of shares without investing a large amount of money.

Monitor the Price Movements of Some Penny Stocks

Because a trader can buy a sizable number of shares, he can generate large profits by taking advantages of daily changes in the price of the penny stock. In addition, through the use of short-term strategies, the investor has to deal with lesser risks.

Don't take your eyes off that Monitor

Penny Stocks can be likened to a game that requires skill, patience, and endurance. The skill required is in spotting trading opportunities at a glance and being able to take advantage of them. You need patience to wait out the market until it makes its move. Sometimes penny stock prices move in a tight range then suddenly start trending going into one direction. You need patience to take advantages of the sudden flurry of activities. Endurance is to be able to withstand tracking the price movements continuously without taking your eyes off the monitor.

Penny stock prices are very volatile and can move very fast. Trading opportunities may appear in one second and will be gone the next. If you as much as blink an eye or get distracted you will lose that chance. This is critical if you are nursing a loss and need to get out at the next best opportunity. And even if you have a winning trade, you will have to take advantage of the next price jump to be able to liquidate your position with a decent profit.

Besides, penny stock trading is so unlike value investing where you buy and hold your position for an extended period of time. With penny stocks, you buy, take your profit on the first significant price jump and run – all in one trading session. This means if you have any open position in the market you can't afford to take your eyes off that monitor.

If you are not in the market though, you should not be up on your toes. There will always be a promising penny stock tomorrow and the next day, and the day after that. Never should you hurry in getting into the market. Choose your battles smartly. The most important thing is you have completed your due diligence and have prepared your game plan ahead.

Avoid the Hype

A lot of penny stock companies are doing artificial means to increase the value of their stock by enticing inexperienced investor to invest in them by buying shares of stock. Because more buyers are getting into the penny stock, it is expected that its price will significantly increase. This is taken advantage of by unscrupulous individuals and businesses by selling their own shares for a much higher price. Thus, traders are advised to make a thorough research first of the business before investing in it. The historical price fluctuations can be analyzed and economic news can be used in order to gauge if the penny stock is a good investment or not.

Use Effective Strategies

To maximize profits and mitigate risks, an individual can trade consistently just one stock and take time to research about the company's business. He can learn quickly and confidently predict any change in value through the use of effective strategies. A lot of penny stock companies have small-scale operations and generate low revenues monthly. These enterprises can easily collapse. As such, it is best to select a penny stock company with a broad customer base. The investor can also choose a company which is into high-demand product and service development.

Analyze Volume

In selecting a penny stock, the trader must choose a business which offer high volume of shares. Top penny stocks can be used for day trading activities if these stocks have thousand of shares at a low price. The person can buy and sell these stocks frequently for short periods of time in order to earn more profits. However, it important to find out if there is a large number of investors and traders who are interested in trading the shares of that company. If there is a high demand for a particular penny stock, the shares can generate substantial profits. By analyzing the trading volume, a trader can choose the best penny stocks for his day trading strategies.

Take Advantage of Volatility

A lot of investors can keep shares of stock for so many years before locking in their profits by selling them. Within this long period of time, the company sells all its assets, be merged with another company, or go out of business. On the other hand, top penny stocks, which are more volatile, can be bought by traders and sold before the trading day ends. The volatility of penny stocks ensures that the traders sell their shares within the day in order to maximize the short-term profits.

Buy the Shares of Stock at the Appropriate Time

If there's sharp drop in the value of a penny stock, a lot of its shareholders will want to sell their shares. Therefore, a large volume of the stock is available for sale at a low price. Once the shares are bought, it is imperative for the trader to monitor the fluctuations of the price until it tops its average daily peak then the shares can be sold for maximum profit.

Learn How to Take Your Loss in a Stride

Penny stock trading is one of the most speculative forms of investments. It entails a great deal of risk. With careful planning and analysis you can make a fortune. With greed and careless abandon you can lose a fortune. Being highly speculative, you should not expect to be able to call the shots correctly all the time. Be prepared to lose some – and when you do just take it in a stride.

Some traders get too personal when they lose a trade – more so if they string successive losing trades. They feel the need to get back at the market. As a consequence, they start to trade with wanton abandon. Quite often, they end up trading with their gut and not with the brain. They lose their objectivity and start trading on impulse. This is when the market swallows them up - hook, line, and sinker.

Such a scenario is often the result of trading with money you can't afford to lose. Say for example if what you invested on penny stocks is money meant for the college education of your kid, you will surely try to run after the market when you lose your first trade in an effort to regain your loss. And when you get a string of losses, you'll definitely end up a nervous wreck – smarting from the loss and even losing sleep over it.

On the other hand, if you trade with money you can afford to lose, you'll be able to remain calm and compose ready to trade the next trading opportunity that comes around. It is imperative that you learn how to take a loss in a stride. And the only time you can do that is if you trade with risk money – money you can lose without worry.

Chapter 9: Learn How to Use Penny Stock Level 2 Quotes to Reveal the Underlying Market Sentiment

One important trading tool every penny stock investor cannot afford not to have is the Penny Stock Level 2 Quote. Compared to regular quotes which give you merely the bid and ask price of the stock and sometimes the trading volume too, the Penny Stock Level 2 Quotes is like letting you view what is going on under the hood.

With Penny Stock Level 2 Quotes, you'll be able to know how many are selling as well as how many are buying a particular stock at any given time. It will even tell you if a market maker is pushing the price towards a particular direction – up or down. With it, you will also be able to discern with great ease the price levels where the market makers start entering the market to support a certain price they want to protect as well as the price levels where they start shorting the stock.

The Penny Stock Level 2 Quotes gives you an accurate account and a clear grasp of the ongoing trading activities. You will be able to see every trade and every order in real time and how each order impacts the price. This is an important piece of trading information considering that with penny stocks, prices can soar with just a few orders. These quotes allow you to read the prevailing market sentiment throughout the trading session.

In penny stock trading there is always one market maker who practically dictates the tempo and the direction of the trading on a particular stock. They call this market maker the ax. Using the Penny Stock Level 2 Quotes, you'll not only be able to identify who the ax is and where he wants to take the price.

Penny Stock Level 2 Quotes is usually provided for free by online brokers. The liquidity of penny stock trading may be low and therefore can be influenced by a market maker but with the Penny Stock Level 2 Quotes providing you detailed information on every price move, you don't have to guess your way around to profit. All you need to do is trade along with the ax on a trending market and you'll surely string some profitable trades.

Market makers may try to disguise their moves by breaking down their orders in tranches and course them through several brokers using the Electronic Communication Network (ECN) but this won't be difficult to determine. You can use Penny Stock Level 2 Quotes together with other real time charting tools like the candle stick charts and nothing can be hidden from you. If you have had some experience in trading before, this should not be a problem. It may however require some learning curve for beginners.

If this is the first time for you to trade stocks, the best advice is to do some paper trading first. Some brokers allow you to mock trade using a virtual account with virtual money. You should take this opportunity to acquire hands-on trading experience to familiarize yourself with the mechanics of stock trading as well as expand your knowledge on the use of Penny Stock Level 2 Quotes.

Chapter 10: Choosing a Penny Stock Broker

Selecting a Penny Stock Broker

A penny stock broker facilitates trading by offering the required trading platform for investors and traders. He can also influence the trading patterns, preferences, and behaviors of the stakeholders by providing sales, marketing, and recommendations. As such, it is important for a trader or investor to choose the right broker for his penny stocks investment.

A lot of these brokers now provide online and mobile trading platforms. A dematerialized account is a depository of the investor's shares while the nostrum is the bank account for trading shares. Only a few brokers provide nostrum facilities. Since penny stock trading is highly speculative in nature, prices can fluctuate erratically.

Reliable and instant money transfers are required for timely and efficient trading at desired prices. An investor may suffer significant losses if there are bottlenecks in the transfer of money. Therefore, it is best for him to choose a broker who provides both nostro and depository facilities.

In the case of penny stocks, transactional costs play a major role. It is important for the investor to know about transaction charges, which can easily be found on the broker's website. The individual must also take particular notice of additional terms and conditions listed on the site.

Some brokers may charge a minimum brokerage fee per share. This means that an additional fee per share may be charged to the investor for every transaction. For example, a $0.10 stock with $0.03 minimum brokerage fee per share will cost about $0.13 per share. For 10,000 shares of a penny stock, the investor will have to pay $300 more than the present market price.

Some brokers may also charge a minimum brokerage fee per order. For example, a 1,000 shares of penny stock with current market price of $0.01 and 3% brokerage or $10 minimum brokerage fee per trade order will cost the investor $10.30. However, since $0.30 is less than $10, the investor will have to pay the $10 minimum brokerage fee. Thus, he will pay $20 for the transaction.

A broker may also set additional charges for large orders. This large order surcharge will apply if the investor buys shares which are more than the maximum shares set by the broker. In addition, the broker can also set monthly minimum trades. If an investor fails to meet the required number of trades, he may be charged an additional fee.

There is also an annual maintenance fee which is charged by brokers for every trading account. Additional charges may also include fees for money transfers, depository accounts, etc. Some brokers also require a minimum deposit to open a penny stock trading account. Furthermore, they also charge additional fees for accounts which have been inactive for a long time. They may also charge a withdrawal fee every time money is transferred from the trading account to the investor's bank account.

There are brokers who don't allow short-selling of stocks. If an investor wants to short sell penny stocks, he must search for a broker who offers that service. It must be noted that short selling needs maintenance of a higher margin amount. Because trading penny stocks is highly volatile, any trader who short sells this type of stock must be ready to deposit additional margin money at short notice.

Because of the price volatility of penny stocks, the hold time on the phone and the response time of the website are top considerations. An investor needs to enter or exit a position in real time because prices can change quickly. If he needs different customer services like reports and research tools, technical indicators, and data feeds, it is important that he ask his broker about their costs because most of these services are offered for a high fee.

Now, before you start looking for an ideal penny stock broker you will be working with you need to set your investment goals and trading strategies first because you need to tailor-fit your goals and strategies with the characteristics of the brokers you choose.

For example, if you intend to trade small like just a few hundred green bucks, you would be better off trading with a broker who does impose any minimum initial balance requirement. If on the other hand, you intend to engage actively in trading churning over 20 buy and sell transactions each week, then you will be better off with a broker who charges very minimal commissions.

Here is a questionnaire you can use to find out which broker you should include in your shortlist as well as determine if your shortlisted brokers matches your purpose, strategies, and investment goals to a tee:

- Does he require an initial minimum deposit to open an account?

- Does he impose penalties if your account balances hits a certain low level?

- How much commission fees does he charge per trade?

- Does he have special commission rates for lower-priced shares?

- Does he have restrictions on trading certain markets?

- Is his trading platform user friendly and easy to learn?

- Does he provide prompt customer services both phone and e-mail?

- Are there provisions for research and analysis tools embedded in the trading platform?

- How fast and accurate are the trade executions?

- How big is his client base?

This questionnaire will help you decide which criteria will be important to you in choosing your ideal broker. You should however do some background research on your potential brokers before you make up your mind which discount broker who best meets your needs.

Don't hesitate to change your Broker

If your existing broker does not meet up to your expectations, go ahead and change him immediately. There are plenty of brokers out there just waiting for your call. Besides, you really should not place all your trades through a single broker. So, don't be afraid to make a changeover if your current broker does not deliver as expected. It is your money on the line and not his.

The ideal way is to have an account with a broker with the best trading platform; another account exclusively for trading penny stocks; and a third account for trading equities in larger volumes.

Chapter 11: People Who Earned Millions from Penny Stocks

Joshua Sason

When Joshua Sason was still 21 years old, he lived with his parents and dreamt of becoming a rock star. He had a boring job at a Long Island law firm, which specializes in debt collection. His friend taught him a legal and rare trick that made him a millionaire through his penny stock investments. Some critics will say that his story is just for advertisements but it is really a true-to-life story.

Although Joshua doesn't want to share his secrets, he left a paper trail. A lot of companies had regulatory filings and it showed that Joshua's company, Magna, had at least $200 million in penny stocks since 2012. Today, he's enjoying his life with his model girlfriend and hanging out with movie stars. He's actually producing a movie with Martin Scorsese.

Joshua, although notoriously tight-lipped, is a self-taught value investor. He doesn't want to give away his secrets but tells people that he creates businesses and dabbles into investments as well. For sure, he has complex trading strategies and finds a way to invests in companies, which are nearing bankruptcy. Currently, his company, Magna, has at least 80 investments.

Joshua Sason is able to close deals which allow him to profit significantly by turning debts into equity at a preset discount. 71 of these companies had shown a drop in value but he's still making money from them. He gets his penny stock investments for less money. Magna plays a dominant role in penny stock trading. It's very similar to a pawnshop for penny stocks.

Some of his investments had company executives, who were charged with fraud. Joshua lends money to these companies in exchange for a significant number of shares of stock. Although these companies know that the sell off are bad for their stockholders, Magna invests in them if the price of the stock declines lower prior to dumping them.

Considered by critics as "death-spiral financing", Joshua often makes at most 10 times more than his original investment in just a few months. The public may believe that the scheme is illegal but it's not. A lot of Ivy League-type investors and hedge funds don't want to try penny stocks investing because they are uncomfortable about the securities law's loopholes. Some investors, if they're not careful, may exploit these loopholes and err on the side of fraud. However, Joshua knows his game and has remained on the right side of the law. He had not encountered problems with regulators.

Tim Grittani

Tim Grittani amassed wealth from trading penny stocks with a $1,500 capital. Although very risky, he admitted that his success has been a slow, day-to-day process. His entire day is spent in from of the computer. He transacts penny stocks at the right time. In some cases, he has entered and exited a position within minutes. He rarely holds his penny stock shares for a few days.

Trading penny stocks is highly speculative because most of them are thinly traded and transacted over the counter. The Securities and Exchange Commission had issued warnings in the past for investors because they can lose all of their capital. In addition, penny stocks are notorious for pump-and-dump schemes. However, Gritanni raked in a lot of profits because of the market of penny stocks is inefficient. He knows what to search for and recognizes that he can make a lot of money from these pump-and-dump schemes without being part of such plans.

He was able to push his portfolio's value to at least $1 million when he short sold the shares of a company, which had been used by pump-and-dump schemes. He borrowed shares from his broker then sold them. He intended to buy these shares later when the price declines. He followed Nutranomics and noticed that the price increased significantly. He suspected that it was being manipulated by scammers. When he realized that it was losing momentum, he felt that a small recovery was about to take place. Within 23 minutes, the stock lost 60% of its value. He earned $8,000 within 10 minutes.

Tim Grittani considers Tim Sykes as his mentor. Tim Sykes became famous when he turned his $12,000 into millions by trading penny stocks. He's been teaching his strategies through video lessons and instructional newsletters.

Grittani started with $500 when he opened a trading account. He lost half of his money within a few weeks so he sought outside help. He chanced upon the story of Syke on the internet. He learned the theories of trading from Sykes before trying again. Although the first few months was very difficult, he did made some progress within 6 months.

He received an email which targeted Amwest Imaging. He invested $3,000 into it. Since he knew that the scheme will soon collapse, he sold his shares within 10 minutes to lock in his profits of $2,000.

Conclusion

Thank you again for downloading this book!

I hope this book was able to help you to learn how to earn money from trading penny stocks.

The next step is to try the concepts you learned from this book and start your way towards your first million.

Finally, if you enjoyed this book, then I'd like to ask you for a favor, would you be kind enough to leave a review for this book on Amazon? It'd be greatly appreciated!

Thank you and good luck!

Sofia

Made in the USA
San Bernardino, CA
05 April 2016